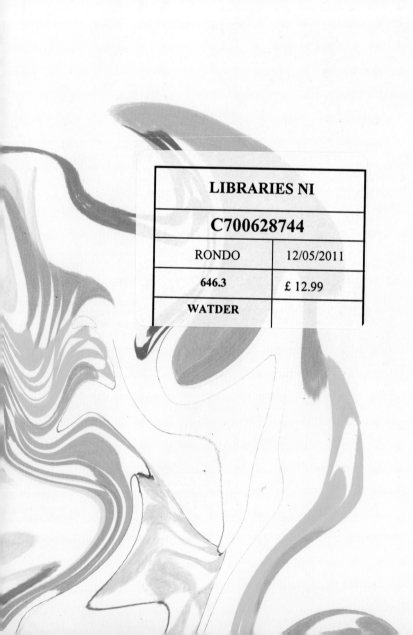

WHAT ON EARTH ARE YOU WEARING?

Dear Michi

I am trying to get a break in the fashion industry but
I keep putting my foot in it, muddling my galloons
with my galoshes, my mules with my muffs. Is there
some kind of book or something that I can get to help
me bluff my way in? Like those cheat notes we had
in school maybe?

Failing that, do you have any positions vacant?

Foot in the Door
Fitzroy,
Australia

Dear Foot in the Door,

Please don't feel bad — these are common
mistakes. I mean, what girl doesn't get her muff
muddled sometimes? I know you may find this hard
to believe, but I was once ignorant of the
fashionisms required to get by in this industry.
In fact, I found the words used around me so
confusing that I started making notes just to
get by. After a while I had enough cheat notes
to fill a book. I was going to photocopy them
for you but then I had a great idea — why not
fill a book? So here it is, a Michipedia of all
my wisdom. I hope it helps.

Yours with encouragement,

michi

P.S. As if I'd give a job
to someone who mixes mules
and muffs, what do you
take me for, an idiot?

What on earth are you wearing?

A MICHIPEDIA OF FASHION

APPLE

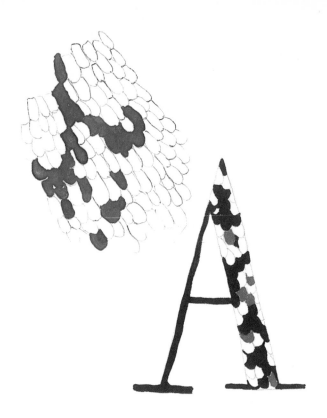

ANIMAL PRINT

Fabric print that turns any 50-something
bar-hopping Botox-loving single woman into an
animal. Most animal-print wearers are not that
fussy about the animal, as long as the result is
horizontally satisfactory.

ANIMAL PRINT

ACID WASH
REFLUX DISEASE

First discovered in the early to mid-80s, Acid Wash Reflux Disease (AWRD) affects nearly one in every four people. The disease is mainly caused when an acid-wash item re-enters a person's life after years in remission. Symptoms include a burning sensation in the stomach, particularly when faced with an acid-wash jacket or jeans. Even old photos or being exposed to revived 80s fashion tragedies can cause immense discomfort. Most at risk are those born in the 70s who experienced acid wash the first time around. Even if a person has never worn acid wash before, it doesn't mean they're in the clear. Medical experts suggest if you've ever been to a White Snake or Bon Jovi concert you should get tested immediately.

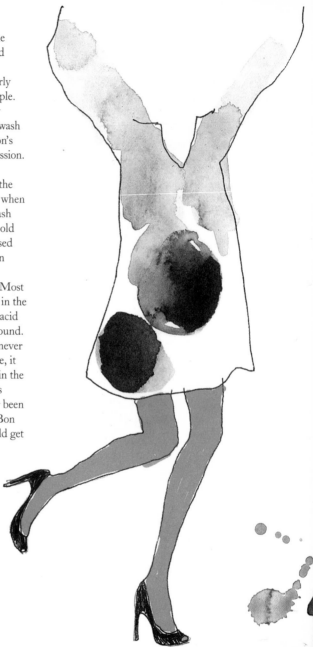

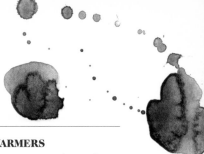

APPLIQUÉ

Lace, beading, sequins, rhinestones, you know, all that decorative stuff. Take some of these, add more, go on and on and appliqué is what you have.

ALOHA SHIRT

The shirt favoured by American tourists that greets you loudly as it enters the room. 'Aloha!'

ANORAK

A lesbian parka.

APRON DRESS

Some call it a pinafore, others call it a way to keep a wife at a sink.

APPAREL

The pretentious word industry folk use for clothes.

ARM WARMERS

Leg warmers worn by punks and Goths too subversive to dress like a sissy dancer.

ADJUSTABLE BACK

The ability to tuck back fat into the top of your togs.

ARMANI

The difference between Katie Holmes and Katie Holmes-Cruise.

ATTRACTIVE

A prerequisite for joining the fashion industry and the very reason why I am merely a bystander.

ACADEMIC DRESS

A really, really smart gown that has a better vocabulary than you do.

BERET

The beret originated in France around the same time
baldness and oily hair were invented. And just like
many other French words, beret comes from the Latin
word *birretum*, which literally means 'just because you
have a stupid floppy cap on your head we all know
you're bald'. Recent studies show that 89% of
non-French people would rather wake up with
a spider on their head than a beret.

BERET

BLOOMERS

A modest undergarment intended to preserve the decency of Victorian women in the 1850s. Now sold to horny businessmen in vending machines in Japan.

BOLERO

A short jacket for people without torsos.

BOTOX

See me in a few years.

BOX PLEAT

A neatly folded vagina.

BAD HAIR DAY

First day at the beach after a long wax-free winter. Unless of course mohair bikinis are suddenly fashionable.

BRAZILIAN

Mass rainforest clearing.

BALENCIAGA

Described by Christian Dior as 'the master of us all'. Described by me as 'the master of my credit card'.

BELT

Waist creator.

BENETTON

Controversial ads, boring clothes.

BIAS CUT

A technique used by designers to ensure mere mortals can't wear their clothes. 'This jumpsuit only comes in size 0, that's a bit bias.'

BOY-LEG KNICKERS

Something designed for boys yet worn by girls due to comfort
and ample hip coverage. The trend for cross-gender undergarments
is not so readily discussed when referring to men in girls' undies.
I wonder why?

BARNEYS

Where good people
go when they die.

Browsing beautiful bikinis at Barneys while
beanstalky bimbos with Brazilians
befriend ~~boys~~ boys bearing
Balenciaga bags.

BIKINI SHOPPING

Fun for some, torture for most. Also known as S&M.

B-CUP

A smaller than average vessel used by bees from which to drink.

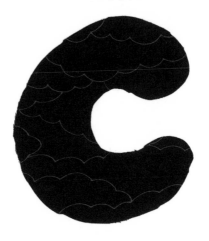

CHICKEN FILLETS

The breast friends of an A-cup.

CHICKEN FILLETS

CACHAREL

The clothing
equivalent of a lover.

CHIC

Pronounced *sheik*,
also someone I once
wrote a letter to
asking for money.

CHANEL
Old money.

CASHMERE
A type of wool made
from cash.

COORDINATE
Boring.

COCAINE
Nose makeup. 'I'm just
going to the bathroom
to powder my nose.'

CRASS
See *Box Pleat*.

COUTURE
Something you can't
afford and even if you
could you probably
wouldn't have anywhere
to wear it.

COAT
Big jacket.

C-CUP
Short for Compromise
cup. 'I'd like to go up to
a D but I guess I'll take
these Cs instead.'

CRIMINAL
Double denim, mustard,
corduroy skirts, skorts,
skousers, overalls,
scrunchies, polo shirts
with collars up, lycra
shorts in public, tracksuit
pants in public, suits
with running shoes.

CHEAP
Pronounced *crap*.

CALVIN KLEIN
Big in underpants and
softcore porn.

Dear Michi,

I recently returned from Hong Kong on a shopping trip with my friends. We had a great time but my experience was left a little marred after I discovered the Chanel bag I purchased was a fake. When I went back to confront the guy on the street who sold it to me, he said it was a genuine 'Channel'. I tried telling him Chanel doesn't have two Ns but he said it did. Either I can't spell or this guy knows something I don't. Please help.

Hoodwinked
Hampstead Heath,
London, UK

Dear Hoodwinked,

I'm sorry to tell you this but the man on the street was telling the truth. Born in the early 70s to humble factory workers Louis Veeton and Donna Kebab, Cocoa Channel quickly made a name for herself in the fast fashion industry sewing upside-down crocodiles on polo shirts at her uncle's Lacrock factory. After a number of successful apprenticeships with Klowey and Versarchi, Cocoa then went on to develop the iconic car boot retail system, which can still be seen today on high streets and back alleys around the world. In the early 90s Cocoa launched the iconic Channel brand. Often mistaken for the popular Parisian fashion house Chanel, the Channel label can be identified by the famous interlocking double horseshoe logo, which can be seen on everything from bags to jackets as well as Cocoa's hugely successful Channel No.6 perfume.

Commiserations,

 x x

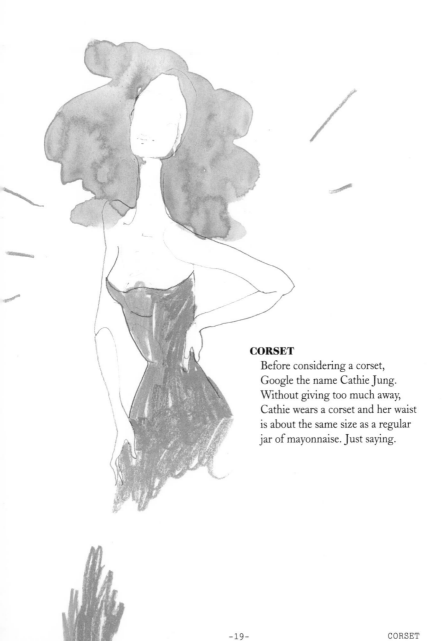

CORSET

Before considering a corset,
Google the name Cathie Jung.
Without giving too much away,
Cathie wears a corset and her waist
is about the same size as a regular
jar of mayonnaise. Just saying.

DEBT

Nice wardrobe.

hristian Dior

Drain Ostrich

d Ironic Shit

adio Rich Nits

DÉCOLLETAGE

Said Captain Peacock to Mrs Slocombe: 'Do you have a pen Mrs Slocombe?' 'Certainly Captain Peacock, I'll just retrieve it from my décolletage.'

DAISY DUKES

Really short denim shorts. 'Gee, those Daisy Dukes are tiny, it looks like they're going right up her crack like denim dental floss.'

DEMI TOE

A toe that bears an uncanny resemblance to Ashton Kutcher's wife. 'Ouch, I just stubbed my Demi…I think she's broken.'

DOC MARTENS

Not really a doctor.

DOLCE & GABBANA

The only two guys in the world who can get away with a golden mosaic shower.

DONNA KARAN

Double front-name designer. Will answer to Donna or Karan. Or Ms Karan. Or DK. But not Kazza.

DOTTED SWISS

1) Sheer cotton fabric embellished with woven, flocked or embroidered raised dots.
2) Swiss teen going through puberty.

DRESS

Are you sure this book's for you?

DWAYNE PIPE

Midwest stylist who created the overalls and toothpick-in-mouth look.

DRIES VAN NOTEN

Usually anything involving a 'van' is dodgy. This is the one exception to that rule.

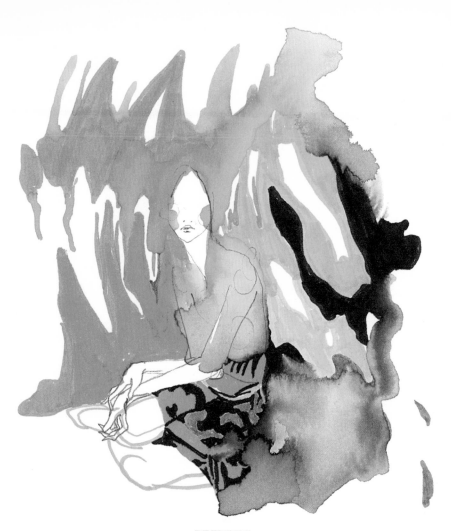

DEZIGNER

Abiding by the international dezign code of 'more is more',
the dezigner will use everything at his or her disposal to
catch your eye. More colours, more textures, more beads,
more puffy paint, more everything. The most common type
of dezigner is the 'in-house fashion dezigner', someone who
owns a bedazzler and works predominantly from their
kitchen table. See www.etsy.com for more.

DESERT BOOTS

Cute boots from my childhood made from suede. Not to be confused with *dessert boots*, which are boots made from cake.

DOUBLE D-CUP

Greedy. If only Mother Nature was a Communist we'd all get a piece of that action.

DRAWSTRING WAIST
Evidence that you're
probably eating too
much.

EMBELLISHED

Material or clothing that has been decorated with rhinestones, buckles, buttons, bows, embroidery. Best left to children.

ELASTIC WAISTBAND

Go to Krispy Kreme much?

ELEGANT

Easier said than done.

ETON COLLAR

A large stiff turnover collar on a large stiff.

ETHICAL WEAR

A concept that should stay in our minds for years to come. Unless of course we lose our short-term memory after smoking all our hemp trainers.

EYELASH LACE

A lace garment with
eyelash strands at the edges.
Best left to porn stars.

EYELASH LACE

ESPADRILLE /
ES-PA-DRILLE

A shoe with a canvas upper and rope sole.
Slap whomever you see wearing them – they are lost
and confused. Only last year it was reported that
Mr and Mrs Howell, former residents of Gilligan's
Island, were seen in espadrilles tidying racks
in the resort section of Macy's Miami.

EASY FIGURE FIXES
A fashion phrase that
can be loosely
translated as 'hide
your fat under A-line
skirts and smock tops'.

EARMUFF

Porn position.

EARTH TONES

A nice way of saying brown.

EARTHY

A nice way of saying dowdy.

ECRU

A nice way of saying brown and dowdy.

EGYPTIAN COTTON

Posh sheets stolen from hotels.

ENVELOPE POCKET

A pocket for envelopes.

EYELET

Handy when you're busting or have just picked up Javier Bardem.

EARFLAP

A covering for the ears to drown out out the sounds of your kin when huntin' and fishin'.

EPAULET

An ornamental shoulder piece that is not a parrot.

EMPIRE WAIST

Insert Benny Hill theme song here.

ELBOW PATCH

An effective way to tell the staff from the students at posh universities.

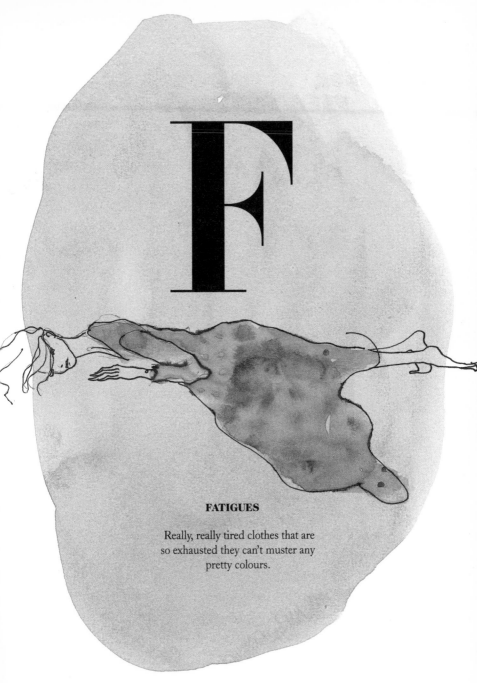

F

FATIGUES

Really, really tired clothes that are
so exhausted they can't muster any
pretty colours.

FOR FREDDIE her French FANNY Pack FLEA MARKET was FASCINATING FOR it felt FLAT AGAINST FANNY, BUT HER FURRY FAUX FUR is FAR MORE FUN, FLEECY & FORMAL

FAUX FUR
  It's okay, until the faux
  becomes endangered.

FANNY PACK
  A small pouch worn
  by people without any
  self-respect.

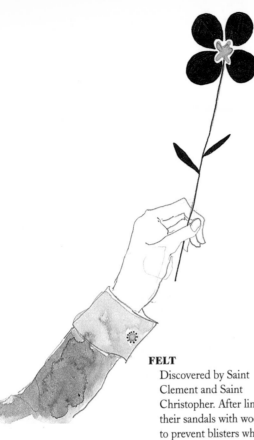

FRENCH CUFF
A smoking hot Frenchman who ties up your sleeves.

FACONNE
French for 'fancy weave'. Sounds even fancier when spoken by a Frenchman.

FELT
Discovered by Saint Clement and Saint Christopher. After lining their sandals with wool to prevent blisters while fleeing persecution, at the end of their long journey, they realised the sweat had turned the wool into felt socks. But what's more disgusting is that this discovery also led to the 'sock and sandal' phenomenon, which is still practised by many Germans today. Saints? I think not.

FACONNE

FLOCKING

Flocking dates back to 1638, when Louis XIV of France became addicted to furry wallpaper and slogan T-shirts. The most famous was his 'Get Flocked!' tee, immortalised in this 1670 painting by Anon.

FLEA MARKET

1) A place to buy stuff from dead people.
2) A shopping mecca for siphonapteras and other wingless parasites.

FASCINATOR

Proof that not everyone owns a mirror.

FICHU

Bless you! A light triangular scarf for ladies.

FISHNETS

A coarse open-mesh stocking used for catching men or straddling poles.

FLAX

The fibre guilty of making linen.

FLEECE

A sheep's coat. 'Baaaabara, your coat is missing. I think you've been fleeced.'

FOOTWHERE

Term used by large people on documentaries who haven't seen their feet for some time.

FORMAL WEAR

Rented dinner jackets worn by teenagers who have spent all their money buying a cane with a hidden drinking flask inside.

FUR

Worn by animals.

F.O.B. (FRONT ON BREAST)

Tailoring term used to describe positioning of pockets. As in a F.O.B. watch that is worn on a chain tucked into the breast pocket of a waistcoat. 'Do you have the time, Jeeves?' 'Yes, Madame, it's half past my nipple.'

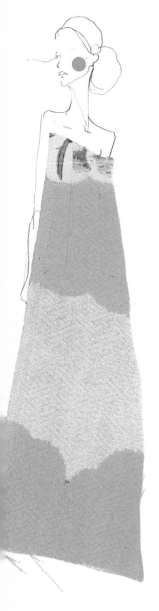

g

GOWN

A versatile term used
to describe a garment
that can take you from
the red carpet or
school prom to the
bedroom, or even to
the hospital. Just like
a gigolo, it'll be
whatever you want
it to be. Baby.

GALLOON

Ornamental braiding used on military
uniforms and furniture. Popularised by the
cult 1960s television series *The Adventures
of Officer Ottoman & Constable Couch*.

GINGHAM

Checked pattern mainly kept to tablecloths and buxom ladies called Maryanne lost on desert islands.

GUSSET

A diamond-shaped piece of fabric. If I stopped there it would sound quite lovely. The fact is, however, that a gusset is sewn into the crotch of knickers for extra strength as this is seen as an area subject to stress. Now, if I were a piece of fabric in a pair of knickers I would be the victim of stress, not the cure. Along with 'moist', 'gusset' is I think the worst word in the English language. And look at that, I have managed to get the words 'moist', 'gusset' and 'crotch' into one paragraph. I'm going to Oxford English's version of hell for sure.

GARTER

A piece of elastic only removable with the teeth of a groom or paying customer.

GOLDFISH HEELS

Wipe-clean Perspex
heels made popular
by the 1997 skin flick
A Whore Called Wanda.

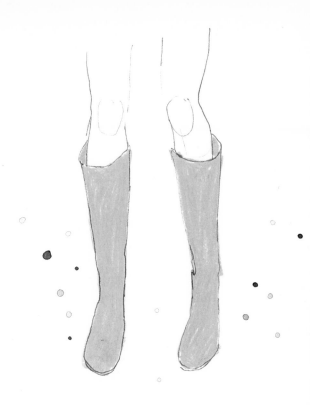

GALOSHES

Terribly posh-sounding
rubber boots made
popular by Paddington
Bear and Kate Moss.

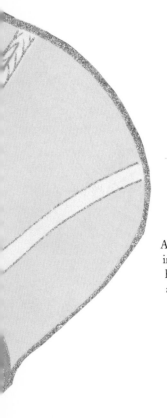

HOUSE DRESS

A modest dress consisting of three rooms,
including a roomy living area around the
hips, two smaller rooms at arms' length,
and a comfortable courtyard at the rear.

HOUSE DRESS

HEMP

Natural bast fibre *(Cannabis sativa)* used in the production of high fashion. 'That dress is amazing, dude.' 'That's not a dress, it's a tree. And I'm not a dude, I'm a talking cat.'

HERRINGBONE

A suiting material made up of parallel lines that resemble the skeleton of a herringbone fish. Originally known as 'dead fish fabric', it didn't really take off until it was rebranded herringbone. Can't think why.

HIKINI

High-cut bikini for those who want the appearance of longer legs. Maybe Sherilyn Fenn should have worn one in *Boxing Helena*?

HIPSTER

1) Someone who values independent thinking, counter-culture, progressive politics, alternative music and creativity.
2) Knickers that show off your bum crack.

HOOD

A soft covering for the head used for robbing banks.

HOOK AND EYE

A simple fastening system used to prevent men from removing bras.

HOT PANTS

Short shorts that look hot on some people, but cold on others.

HIGH HEELS

From the Latin term *altus heelius*, meaning, 'I can see your bald patch from up here.'

HOUNDSTOOTH

A textile pattern that looks more like frogs than dogs' teeth.

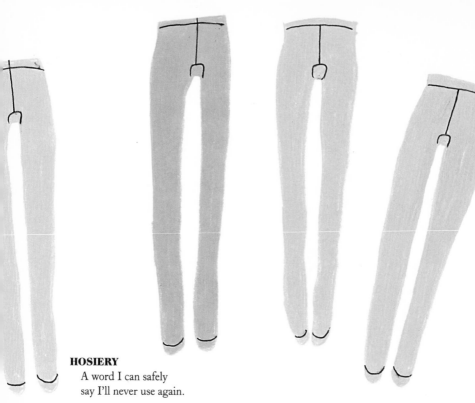

HOSIERY

A word I can safely
say I'll never use again.

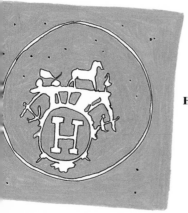

HERMÈS

When I'm kidnapped
and blindfolded with
a silk scarf and then
stuffed into a leather
travel bag, I choose
Hermès.

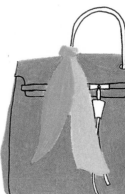

HANDBAG
A sack generally
costing more than
its contents.

HANDBAG

Dear Michi,

Have you seen my keys?

Housebound
Sydney, Australia

Dear Housebound,

Nope, sorry.

Nichi x x

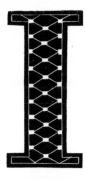

INSEAM

The seam on the inside of the pant leg and the most uncomfortable to measure for a seamstress. 'Please, sir, could you spread 'em a little further? I just need to get as close to your family jewels as possible without actually touching them. Oh, would you look at that, not as big as I thought.' Recent studies show that men never visit the same seamstress twice.

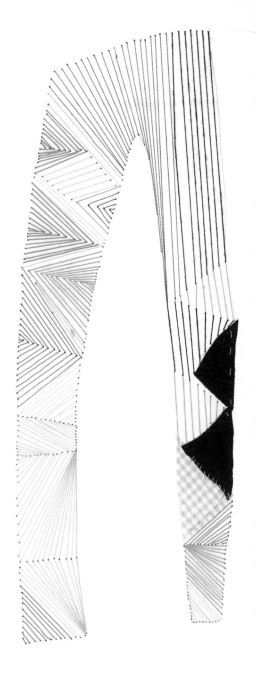

IRON GREY

Created by adding a dash
of green to grey. Leaves
you feeling flat.

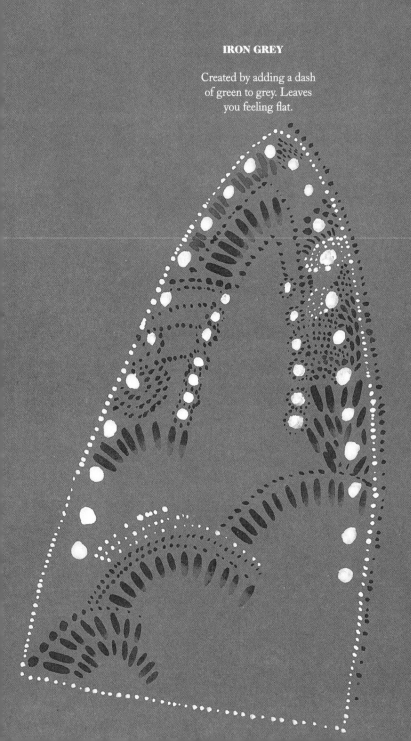

INDIGO

There have been whole books written about
the amazing indigo. Even the Bible mentions it.
As the oldest dye known to man it was used in the
tabernacle of the Ark of the Covenant and all the
way throughout history to Levi's blue jeans.
Natural indigo is the fastest-acting dye known
to man. Hence the name. Go Indi, go!

INDIGO

INKLE

1) A coloured linen tape used for trimming.
2) South African term for ankle.

INVERTED PLEAT

Pleats that reverse the fold of the box pleat. See *Box Pleat* and tell me if you're also thinking of man bits.

IRREGULARS

Read: broken, shoddy, wrong or plain crap. But look how cheap!

ILLUSION

French silk tulle popular for wedding veils. Looks real nice with a carnation and a baby's breath bouquet.

IRIDESCENT

A glowing shininess attracting five-year-old girls to fairy costumes and bugs to bug zappers.

IKAT

A fabric in which the yarns have been tie-dyed before weaving. Also see *Ugly*.

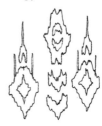

INNER TIE

A hidden tie on the inside of a gown to help keep it closed. Also the hidden businessman within all of us. 'As she read the sales graph she was getting in touch with her inner tie.'

ICE-CREAM

A really long-shot adjective describing the colour cream.

INDIAN RED

A reddish-brown. Who cares though, really? It's not the answer.

JUMPSUIT

Unless you're an astronaut, baby, boilermaker, downhill skier,
plumber, mechanic, racecar driver, skydiver, prisoner or
female truck driver, there's no place for this garment.
You're exempt if you are shaped like a pencil. Bitch.

JACKET

Like a coat but smaller.

JADE

Name for 74% of girls born in the 80s or a bluish-green colour.

JAMBEAU

A piece of medieval armour used to protect the leg below the knee during sale time.

JASPER

A foppish English boy of blackish-green pallor.

JEANS

Like religion and politics, this is a topic my mother told me never to bring up at dinner parties. Too many fundamentalists. For Christ's sake, could one of you Armani-Exchange-wearing, right-winged fascists please pass me the fucking salt?

JOCKSTRAP

Designed for supporting important man bits during vigorous sporting activity, jockstraps consist of a pouch for the genitalia and two elastic straps affixed to the base of the pouch. While all this makes sense, no one can explain to me why the butt cheeks are left exposed. Maybe it has something to do with post-game celebrations?

JOHNNY

1) A short, arse-revealing gown we pay for in hospital.
2) An arse-revealing short man who pays for it anywhere.

JUMPER

A knitted garment a mother makes for her daughter to wear to a birthday party that she was really looking forward to going to because it was at a rollerskating rink. When the daughter saw the jumper it was a hideous poo-brown colour and the wool was so itchy it made her eyes water and her neck come up in red welts. She never ended up going to the party and now every time she hears the word 'jumper' her eyes start to water uncontrollably. Or so I heard from the cousin of a friend of a friend.

JET
1) An intense black.
2) A really fast plane.

JET JET
  A really fast intense
  black plane.

Dear Michi,

Sorry to bother you again, but I still can't find my keys. I seem to have so many things in my pockets I can never find anything. And now I can't leave the house. Can you help me? Please.

Gratefully yours,

Housebound
Sydney, Australia

Dear Housebound,

Have you considered the jackertina? Part suit
jacket, part concertina filing folder, the
jackertina was invented in Sweden in 1982 during
the popular power-suit era. Still common
throughout many parts of Scandinavia today, the
jackertina allows the wearer to dress for success
without being weighed down by a bulky briefcase
or, in your case, housekeys. You can file them
under H, right between Genius and Idiot.

michi x x

KICK PLEAT

Remember *Splash*? That tail had an inverted pleat to get that kick at the end. Not that Darryl is a fake mermaid of course, but if, hypothetically speaking, a human body double were to put on that tail as a costume, she would need an inverted pleat or she couldn't walk. But she could swim really, really well.

KERCHIEF

Square scarf folded in
a triangle, often used
post-cosmetic surgery
to conceal otherwise
impossibly obvious
turkey neck. Best
example of this
kerchief phenomenon
is actress Diane
Keaton, who has not
been seen in public
without a kerchief or
polo-necked sweater
since circa 1974.

KEYHOLE NECKLINE

A shaped hole at the
front of garment.
You can't get in or out
even with a key. Like
a chastity belt for your
boobs. Sort of.
Not really.

KNIFE PLEATS

Really, really sharp
pleats handy for
cutting off wandering
hands.

KNIT FABRIC

Lengthwise ridges
made by knitting are
called Wales.
Crosswise ridges are
called Courses. My
grandmother tried to
teach me to knit when
I was younger. She
had started knitting
socks for a soldier in
WW1 and she
continued the sock in
WW2. When war
broke out in Iraq I
tried to pick up where
she left off. I would
have had more luck
with my wales and
courses if I had done
a course with a whale.

KIDSKIN

Vegans, skip to next
entry. Unless you are
ok in the knowledge
that only very young
goats make such soft
leather.

KINDLY TELL MY KITTY HER KIDSKIN KI
JUST KILLED MY KIMONO-FABRIC KILT
WITH ITS KILLER KEYHOLE.

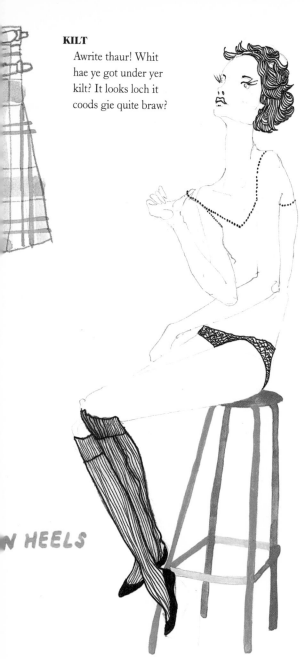

KILT

Awrite thaur! Whit hae ye got under yer kilt? It looks loch it coods gie quite braw?

KNEE-HIGHS

Socks that come to just below the knee, popular with anyone posing as a schoolgirl for men's interest magazines. For reasons unknown to me, men are yet to catch on to the fact that older women do it better and that half stockings are not nearly as useful as half knickers. My next book is called *Why Women are the Superior Gender*.

N HEELS

KITTEN HEELS
Q. How do you make a cat walk?

A. Give her a kitten heel.

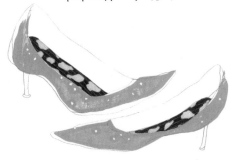

KAWAKUBO, REI

If you don't know the founder of Comme des Garçons then it is quite obvious this relationship will never work.

KENZO

Like Madonna, only one name is needed these days. I mean, do you know anyone else called Kenzo?

KIMONO

Japanese gown tied at the waist. Do you have memoirs of any geishas?

KIMONO SLEEVE

If a kimono sleeve is not big enough, a separate gusset can be added at the underarm. See *Gusset*. Now imagine having your knickers under your arms. Eww.

KABUKI-STYLE

A full-cut, overly dramatic top with dolman-style sleeves (read: baggy) and a collarless square or boat neckline. Or maybe it's a type of sushi?

LACROIX, CHRISTIAN

Sometimes when I want to
look sexy I just mouth the words
'Christian Marie Marc Lacroix'.
Try it in front of the mirror.
Trust me, it works.

LITTLE BLACK DRESS

A simple, elegant black dress that can be dressed up or down depending on the occasion. For example, if you're going to work, pop on some opaques and flats. If you're hocking your box, then it's fishnets and stilettos. The LBD is also standby funeral attire. Be sure to keep away from the fishnets though. Unless, of course, it's your pimp's funeral – then it's probably okay.

LITTLE BLACK DRESS

LACE-UP BOOTS

Popular with dominatrices and guys who served in 'Nam.

LEATHER

Natural material that should be used sparingly because one day the cows will sue us and we'll have to give it all back.

LEOTARD

Worn by six-year-old ballerinas, Madonna and, according to Google image search, a woman known simply as 'Cat Woman Jolene'.

LINGERIE

It's a statistically proven fact that women wear their fanciest lingerie to weddings. Sadly once they've had their own wedding, it's all nanna pants and sports bras. Come on, ladies, let's make more of an effort, shall we?

LATEX

Sometimes it's best just to image search a word on Google. Probably best not to do this one in the office though.

LIPSTICK

Thick red pen used for drawing your face on.

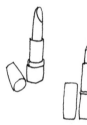

LONG JOHNS

Ankle-length underwear popular in the late nineteenth century and named to make us think that the wearer had a long johnson.

LYCRA

No.

LEOPARD PRINT

Spotty fabric that
looks like one of those
big spotted cats that
I can never remember
the name of.

LACE

LACE
With so many holes,
shouldn't it cost less?

LACE

ME.

MATERNITY BRA

Obviously this is a bra you wear when you're knocked up. A bit like an ex-boyfriend – super important at the time and you can't live without it. Then when you're done, you never want to see it again. Ever.

MESH

Synthetic fabric full of tiny openings like a net. Depending on the size of the opening, mesh ranges from a subtle insert on skimpy lingerie to a ham stuffed in an orange bag.

MERRY WIDOW

A strapless corset with demi cups and garters, coming to a point at the front. Have you got a clear picture of that? Now tell me, what widow wouldn't be merry in that?

MUSCLE SHIRT

A T-shirt popular in suburban malls with males who have the names of their children tattooed on their forearms in ye olde worlde script. Surnames as first names and celebrity children's names are the most common – for example, Tyler, Taylor, Brooklyn, Scout or Bogan.

MERINO WOOL

Merino wool is the wool that is gleaned from the sheep's second or third shearing. Just like your leg hair, the more you shave, the coarser and thicker the wool gets. I am going to start a farm that waxes sheep so that the wool gets finer each time.
In my reverso world I have permanently adolescent sheep and am a billionaire.

MINIMISER BRA

Who knew anyone would want smaller boobs?

MAO COLLAR

A standing collar turned over, named for former chairman Mao Tse-Tung. Given his death tally was almost 20 million people from starvation during 'The Great Leap Forward', I would suggest that fashion and starvation could possibly separate themselves on this one and lose the Mao collar.

MOCK SEAMS

You know seams in the back of stockings are pretty sexy, right? Well, fake ones aren't. Remember that.

MOCK

An imitation of something, as in 'mock fly'. Gee, scary thought if you're busting. 'I really need to go to the loo but it seems my zip is just mock.'

MULE

1) Shoe or slipper, usually made with high heel, bit at the front, nothing at the back.
2) Like a donkey.
3) Drug carrier.
4) Tricky word, none of the answers are that good, are they? Maybe I should have left it out.

MINI SKIRT
A very short skirt. If you bend over
everyone can see your knickers.

MICRO MINI SKIRT
A very, very short skirt. If you bend
over everyone can see lunch.

MISSONI

A big family affair
built on amazing taste
and high prices totally
justified by incredible
colour palettes and
very lovely clothes.
If there is a wedding
registry without some
Missoni homewares
on it, I am not friends
with that couple.

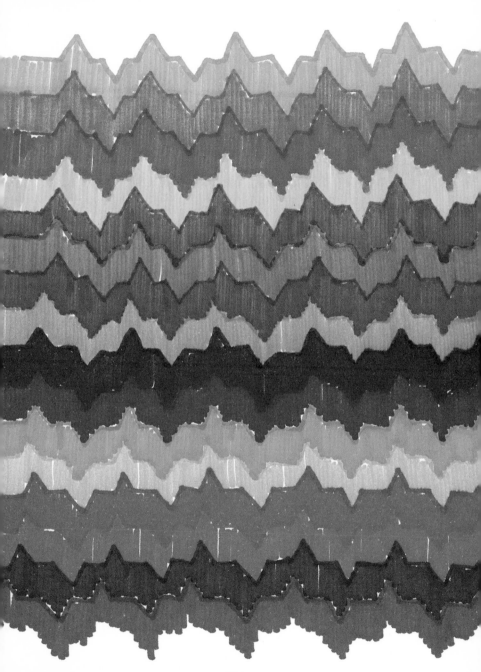

MISSONI

NOT PANTS

Originally designed as riding pants or tights
for notable European men several centuries ago,
not pants were accidentally invented by King
Henry VIII of England when he failed to take
off his tights after a morning riding session.
Preferring the comfort of tight silk or fine wool
against his bottom half, the King had many an
argument with his wife(s) after refusing to
remove his tights when going to the market or
out for dinner. History records show that many
of his wives' last words were, *'For God's sake,
Henry, they're not pants!'*

NOT PANTS

NEEDLE COUNT

1) The total number of needles used in knitting. The higher the needle count, the closer the stitches.

2) The total number of needles found in laneways. The higher the needle count, the cheaper the rent.

NONWOVENS

Clothes made from bellybutton lint.

NOVELTY UNDERWEAR

The underwear equivalent of squirting flowers, whoopee cushions and fake vomit. In other words, you'll never get laid with it.

NYLON

A synthetic material made popular in the 1940s with the invention of stockings. Made less popular in the 1970s with the invention of tight-fitting nylon skirts that would self-combust in front of heaters. In other words, much more exciting than cotton.

NADIA, THE NEEDLE COUNT IN MY
NETTING NEGLIGEE IS
NOTHING COMPARED
TO THE NYLON
ON NETTY'S NOVELTY
NUDE BRA.

NUDE UNDERWEAR
A natural-coloured underwear set that makes it looks like you've got Barbie's bits. Without the disconnecting limbs, of course.

NIPPLE TASSELS
Not surprisingly, there are twice as many nipple tassels than penis tassels in the world.

NINJA SLIPPER
1) Soft slip-on shoe worn by a ninja.
2) A stealth camel toe.

NEGLIGEE

Night attire that says,
'Yes please.'

NIGHTGOWN

Night attire that says,
'No thanks.'

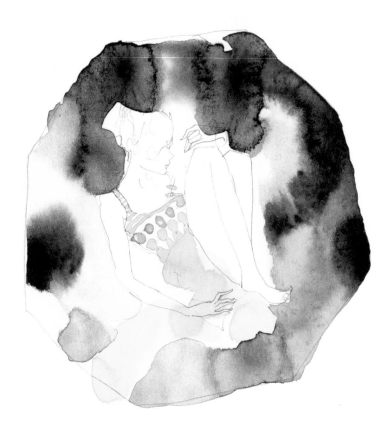

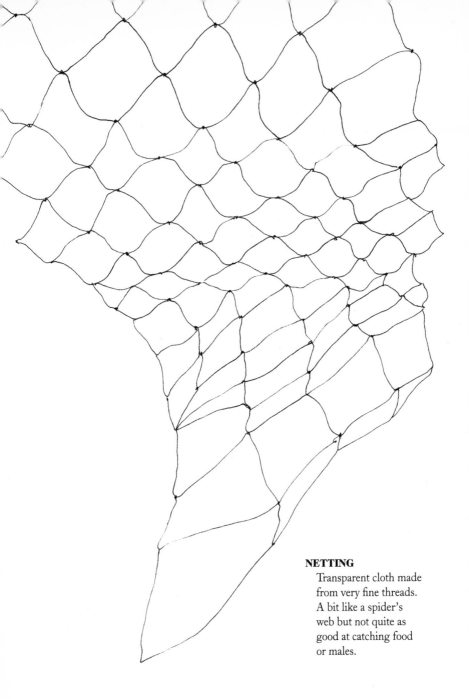

NETTING

Transparent cloth made
from very fine threads.
A bit like a spider's
web but not quite as
good at catching food
or males.

OPERA HAT

A man's collapsible top hat. Not seen nearly
enough these days and something I would
personally like to bring back – if only for
magic's sake.

OPERA HAT

OCHRE

Roll in the dust in the middle of the desert and you got it.

OFF THE SHOULDER

'… and as he slipped it off the shoulder her dress fell silently to the floor. The room was pulsing with electricity …' Oh, sorry, got carried away.

ONE-WAY PLEATS

Pleats all folded in the same direction. If you try to go against the grain they will slice you. Never make a pleat angry, they're unforgiving.

OPEN CROTCH

Buzz not explaining.

ORGANZA

Ask any meringue bride and you'll know it goes perfectly with her gyp and her pearl-finish pumps.

ORGANZINE

1) A raw silk yarn used for warp thread in fine fabrics.
2) A magazine made from hearts and lungs.

OPEN REAR

Pass.

ORANGE

You know this one.

ORANGISH

You almost know this one.

ORANGEY

Resembling something you almost know.

OVERALL

Bib and brace trousers. Favoured by hillbillies, midwest house painters and my best friend, who was wearing overalls when she wet her pants lining up to try and get into a nightclub. Sadly she was 16 at the time, not six.

OYSTER

A greyish-white color. Makes me gag just thinking about the noise a colour like that makes.

OPAQUE
The opposite of sheer.
And the best friend
of anyone with knees
like mine.

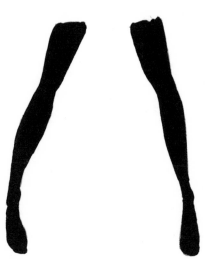

OPAQUE

OLD ROSE
1) Greyish red.
2) A lot of people's
   grandmothers.

OBI

A wide fabric belt tied under the boobs of Japanese women wearing a kimono. Unfortunately adaptations were popular during the 1970s, 1980s and 1990s, with Western women thinking it was okay to wear them on almost any dress. Not condoned by me, and given I am vaguely Japanese I think I can say this with authority.

OBI

PANNE

A lightweight velvet fabric. I'm not sure what you'd use this for but I imagine it would be pretty popular in the Playboy mansion.

PADDED BRA

A bra with padded fiberfill cups designed to add size and definition to those of us with smaller boobs. They may as well put a disabled sign on the outside.

PANTY

I'm currently campaigning to have this word banished from all dictionaries and languages around the world. It's going to take a while, so for the time being let's just say knickers, shall we?

PANTYHOSE

As above.

PATENT LEATHER

When my mum was at school they wouldn't let the boys wear patent-leather shoes because they thought they would use them to look up girls' skirts. I guess this was the Beta version of upskirting.

PLUNGE BRA

Just like a plunge pool, you can just dive right in for a quickie.

PEEKABOO CUPS

A bra that partially exposes the breasts or nipples through a slit or hole. I can't work out what's more gross; that, or the fact that I just wrote a sentence with 'nipple', 'slit' and 'hole' in it. I need to take a bath. Really.

PENCIL SKIRT

A straight, narrow-cut skirt that makes you look like a pencil. Unless of course you have an arse like a watermelon – then it will make you look like a tin of paint.

PETITE-FIGURE BRA

Is 'booblets' a word?

PIPING

Decorative fabric edge found on 70s short shorts and wedding cakes.

PUSH-UP BRA

A euphemism for non-invasive cosmetic surgery.

PASHMINA

A shawl made from a goat. No wonder they came up with another name for it. You'd never wear it if it were called a goat shawl. Come to think of it, I wouldn't wear one anyway.

PEIGNOIR
A posh name
for a see-through
dressing-gown.
Popular with brides,
escorts and ... well,
no one else.

PANTALOONS

A style of men's pants popular in the seventeenth century in England. Not so popular any more, not sure why – it's such a great word, don't you think?

POLYESTER

Polyester was originally discovered in 1940 by British housewife Polly Ester while cleaning up her husband's mess in the shed. The 'mess', consisting of ethylene glycol and terephthalic acid, later formed the basis for the multi-billion-dollar polyester industry which is now used to make everything from pants to plastic bottles.

Unfortunately for Polly, she decided to throw the mess in the bin and missed out on becoming one of the wealthiest women of all time. (Okay, I may have made some of this up but the real story is pretty boring. Trust me, this version is much more interesting.)

Dear Michi,

My boyfriend likes to keep food in his pants. Bananas, chocolate bars, fruit and nut mix; he even once kept a hot roast beef sandwich in his pocket, which he pulled out during a movie. He assures me it's a completely normal thing to do and that in some countries they even have special pants for such occasions. Is he telling the truth or should I dump him like a two-day-old dim sum?

Fed Up
Sheffield, UK

Dear Fed Up,

The idea of keeping food in our pants is nothing
new. Marathon runners have been doing it for
years, and apparently Oprah keeps a chicken
drumstick in her pocket during every show in
case she gets a little peckish. But the pants
your boyfriend is referring to are called
pantries and were invented in Bulgaria in the
late 1970s. Made with specially designed pockets
that lock in the freshness, each pair of
pantries can store up to four square meals and a
variety of snacks and drinks, perfect for those
who like to eat their cake and wear it too. And
as to your question about whether you should
dump your boyfriend? It all depends on whether
he has room in his pants for anything else.

michi x

QUEEN-SIZE

A bigger clothes size than
usual. Sometimes called
plus size but gee, queen
is way nicer.

**QUESTIONABLE
TASTE**
Just ask me.

QIVIUT

A fibre that comes from the hair of the musk ox. Not surprisingly, it is very hard to find. I think I might start breeding this musk ox creature. Sounds like a gold mine to me. I'll just add it to my list of things I am going to invent, along with the cloning machine, a time/space travel shuttle and someone to read to me every night for hours without getting bored.

QUILTING

Just like the club sandwich, only puffier. Three layers – top, padding and lining, all in together with some natty stitching.

WHILE QUIETLY QUILTING
HER QUEEN-SIZED
QUOKKA A CROWN,
QUEEN ANNE
QUESTIONED THE QUICKNESS
~~THE~~ OF HER QUEST FOR
QIVIUT QUILLS.

QUILTING

QUEEN ANNE COLLAR

A collar that rises high
at the back of the neck,
over the shoulders, leaves
a few gaps here. But
apparently does not stop
you from losing your head.
Should perhaps have been
left back in the days of
yore.

RETRO

Lazy rehash.

ROBE

What I would wear all day
if I had a pool house. Or if
I were a crazy cat lady.

RHINESTONES
Simulated diamonds
used to simulate wealth.

RHINESTONES

RIBBED
Fabric that has raised
vertical lines for extra
pleasure.

RAGLAN SLEEVE
The diagonal shape of
the raglan sleeve was
invented in 1854 as a
way of hiding Lord
Raglan's missing arm
which he lost in battle.
I am pretty sure this is
also where the term
'call to arms' came
from. 'Army! Where
are you?'

RAYON
Made from naturally
occurring polymers,
rayon is neither truly
synthetic nor truly
natural. If it were a
person, it would be
Jocelyn Wildenstein.
But a little silkier.
And less cat-like.

RISE
The distance between
the waistband and
the first horizontal
seam on a pair of
knickers. This rise is
indirectly proportional
to the rise in your
boyfriend's pants.

SEQUINS

What's not to love about a sequin?
Shiny, colourful, little, shiny, light-
reflecting, did I say shiny? Oh, but
use sparingly on clothes.

SCANTIES

Friend of Fundies™.

SEERSUCKER

A fabric with a dull, crinkled surface. Most often worn by dull, crinkled people.

SHRUG

A small and indecisive jacket.

SHAPE-ENHANCER

If I said 'waist-nipper' then you would know what this is. Or girdle. Or tummy-tucker. Or fat redistribution. Or honey-baked ham.

SHEER TO THE WAIST

This phrase is used to describe stockings which are see-through to the waist. Does anyone wear stockings that go higher than the waist?

STRING BIKINI

For good bums only, whichever way you split it.

SHELF BRA

Imagine your boobs with a nice curved little shelf under them. Shelf bras are sometimes called balconette bras. I guess this depends on the size required. For example, I would never fill a balcony.

SHIMMY

1) A shortened version of chemise.
2) The action made by a curvy lady who wants somethin' from her man.

SHORTS

There is a three-inch spot between the bottom of the knee cap and mid-calf where the line is drawn between long shorts and short longs. Short longs are to be avoided.

SHELL

A plain, usually sleeveless top. Often puffy. Wearing one makes you a hero. If you're a turtle.

SLIP

An undergarment to ensure others can't see your undies through your dress. Not something you would ever admit to owning, but actually very handy. A bit like a dust-buster.

SILK

If you lived in a cave and I told you that my beautiful silk dress was made by a team of worms, you would make me a deity. 'All hail Queen Michi, Ruler of the Worm!'

SHEEN

Fabric exhibiting notable sheen. The shinier version of Estevez.

SHIRRED

1) Gathered.
2) Drunk 007, 'shaken, not shirred'.

SNAP CROTCH

The crotch of a garment that opens and closes with press-studs or Velcro. 'Excuse me, Javier, while I rip the pubes out of my snap crotch.'

SUSPENDER THONG

Remember Borat?

SKORT

Once upon a time a mummy skirt met a daddy short and had a baby. Perhaps they should have terminated this pregnancy.

SHEEPSKIN

Ask Pamela Anderson.

SAP GREEN

A strong yellow-green.
More poetic than snot
green but essentially
the same thing.

SCARLET
 Bright red.
 Euphemism for slutty.

Dear Michi,

I am, so my friends say, larger than life. As such,
I have a problem with economy seats on aeroplanes
because my heavy hips don't fit between the armrests.

You're a classy lady – surely you can tell me how to
flutter my lids in such a way as to land me in first
class. Otherwise maybe you can suggest some sort of
position that would allow me to squeeze my cuddly
self into a tiny weeny economy seat.

Oh Michi, you're my last hope.

Love,

I Have a Problem
Houston, Texas
USA

Dear I Have a Problem,

I too had a similar problem recently while
trying to keep abreast of the recent bodycon
trend. As a doer not a talker, I worked with
my friends at NASA to develop the space pant™.
Using the same vacuum-seal technology as space
bags, the space pant™ can suck your arse down
to one third of its original size. Simply attach
the specially designed pants to a household
vacuum cleaner and suck out the unwanted air,
ensuring an airtight seal. You can check this
by breathing. If you can still breathe, it's
no good. Start again. Once your arse has been
sucked down to the size (and firmness) of a
walnut, simply detach the hose and disembark.

Happy travels,

michi x x

TEA SHIRT

What your teapot wears in summer
instead of a cosy.

TAFFETA

A lustrous silk-like fabric made from 80s prom ingredients such as stretch limos, Thompson Twins, Depeche Mode, New Order, West Coast Coolers and at least two guys named Corey.

TAP PANTS

Loose-fitting side-cut knickers, tap pants are designed with a vertical seam down the middle. Worn by performers due to their curtain-opening ability.

THERMAL UNDERWEAR

I can't ever imagine being cold enough to wear clothes under my clothes. Wouldn't you just stay inside next to the heater?

TOE RINGS

They make me feel uncomfortable. I don't trust them.

THIRDS

1) An industry term used to describe dodgy hosiery that can't be sold due to snags, holes and other imperfections.
2) A term used when I want to go back for more snags and doughnut holes, which may lead to more imperfections.

TEDDY

When a camisole and knickers are joined together, it's called a teddy. When a gay man has an ample belly and a beard, he's called a bear. So I don't really need to spell out what a teddy bear is, do I?

TEDDIETTE

Like a teddy, but sluttier. Swap the knickers with a g-string and throw in a garter belt and maybe even some devil horns.

THONG

1) A g-string for your bum.
2) A g-string for your foot.

TIE BACK
A garment with ties or laces that fasten at the back.

TIE FRONT
A garment with ties or laces that fasten at the front.

TIE SIDE
I'm pretty sure you've got the idea now.

TULLE

A stiffened lightweight netted fabric used to make wedding veils and ballet tutus. Clearly tulle and I are not well acquainted.

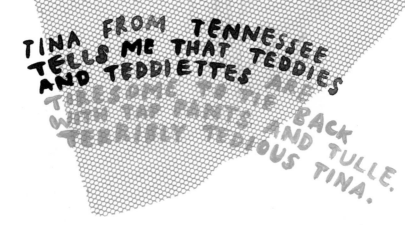

TINA FROM TENNESSEE TELLS ME THAT TEDDIES AND TEDDIETTES ARE TIRESOME TO TIE BACK WITH TAP PANTS AND TULLE. TERRIBLY TEDIOUS TINA.

THIGH-HIGHS

1) Stockings that just reach the mid-thigh.

2) A term used by 80s rock bands who would snort coke off groupies' thighs.

THIGH-HIGHS

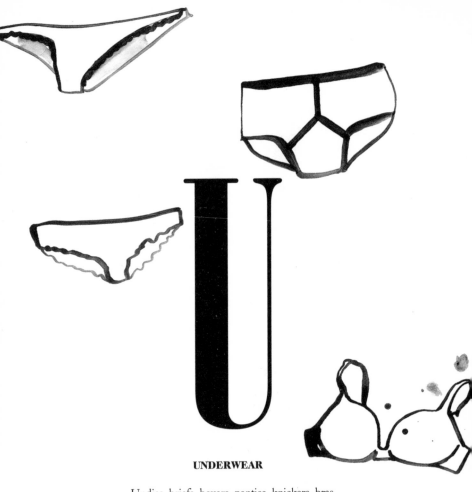

U

UNDERWEAR

Undies, briefs, boxers, panties, knickers, bras,
camisoles, g-strings, things, tightie whities, drawers,
smalls, under roos, nut-huggers, gruds, kex,
cluster-grabbers, butt-huggers, funderwear,
underdaks, bloomers.

UNMENTIONABLES
If you were from the
seventeenth century I would
say see *Underwear.*

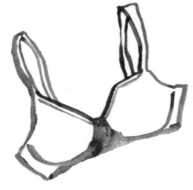

UNITARD

Derogatory term for a close-fitting one-piece all-over garment.

UNION SUIT

Invented for women in Utica, New York, a union suit is an all-in-one flannel suit with buttons down the front and a flap at the back (see *Snap Crotch*) for rest stops. It is impossible to look even vaguely attractive in a union suit. When I wear my union suit I wear a balaclava and break into houses. No one touches an ugly robber.

UNDERWIRE

A strip of flattened steel
wire or similar sewn into
the underside of each
cup of a bra. The visible
difference between with
and without is similar
to the difference between
a fresh tea bag and a
used one.

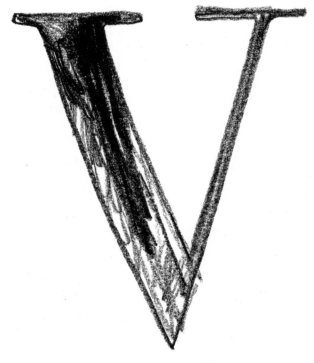

VAMP

The upper part of a shoe
that holds it to the foot.
I wonder if all those heartless
man-eating seductresses know
that they share the same name
as a bit of shoe.

VAMP

VERSACE

Italian fashion label founded by Gianni Versace in 1978. The Versace line covers everything from couture to cosmetics and fragrances to furnishing, but even with all that success poor old Donatella still can't afford to buy a mirror.

VEST

A jacket for people without arms.

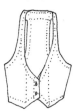

VELOUR

Velvet-like material used to make jackets belonging to geezers who travel in the back of purple limos made from the same fabric.

VELCRO

Invented by Georges de Mestral in 1948 after he discovered why burrs stuck to his pants. Apparently it didn't occur to Georges to wash his pants, or that his new invention was designed to attract almost exclusively pubes and lint. Research shows that to 50-year-old mattress salesmen living in their mothers' basements, the sound of Velcro ripping apart is the most often cited catalyst for matricide.

VELCRO

V-NECK

Acceptable on a T-shirt
or jumper. Not so much
on a pair of pants.

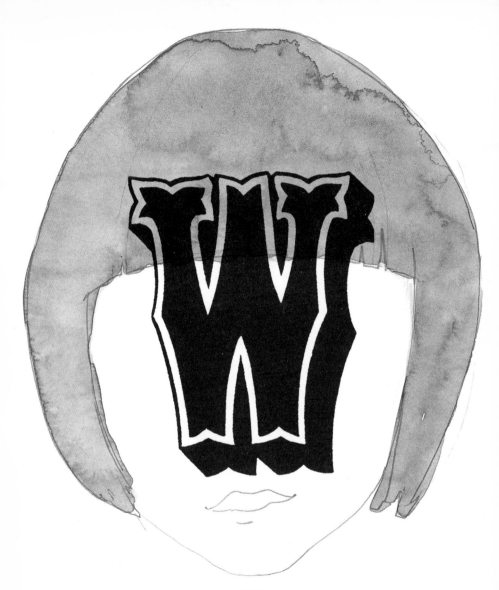

WIG

In the words of a two-year-old
I know, 'a hair hat'.

WAFFLESTOMPER

A hiking boot invented in Brussels in the fourteenth century
as a shortcut for waferers. Rather than using metal-hinged
waffle-pressers, the waferers could just pour their batter
on the ground and stomp it.

WADERS

Gumboots sewn on to waterproof pants. The thought of being able to walk in a straight line through anything without getting wet is extremely appealing to my magical side. I may never wear anything else again.

WARP

Yarns that run the length of the loom at a speed faster than light.

WETSUIT

Rubber suit that surfers wee in before they spend hours in the ocean.

WADMAL

A coarse woollen fabric formerly used in Scandinavia for protective coverings and warm clothing. It is believed the name is derived from a farming couple in the highlands. 'Mal, pass a wad of wool please, I'm freezing my boobs off over here.' And when there was no response, 'Wad Mal! Wad Mal! Wad Mal!'

WHISKERING

The intentional bleach/distress marks on the upper thighs of jeans. The intention is that they should look worn-in from long periods of sitting down. If I were jeans that had to spend so long sitting down I would be naturally distressed. To then be bleached is simply insulting.

WIFE-BEATER

A cotton-ribbed sleeveless singlet with 1950s values and a misogynistic standpoint.

WEDGE

If you don't know the verb *to wedge*, you must be an only child.

WEDGE

X

XXL

A whole lotta lovin'.

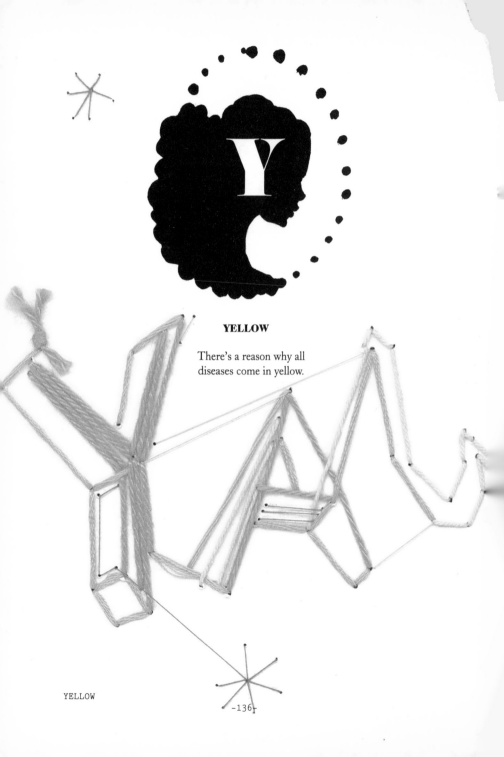

Y

YELLOW

There's a reason why all diseases come in yellow.

YAWN
What usually follows
after I hear the words
'new black'.

YARN
Yarns are made by
twisting fibres together.
I could go on and on
about it but I hate a
boring yarn.

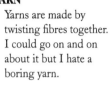

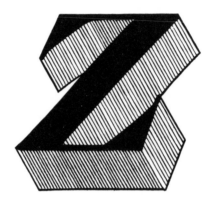

ZEBRA

Zebras were doing
stripes way before
Coco Chanel.

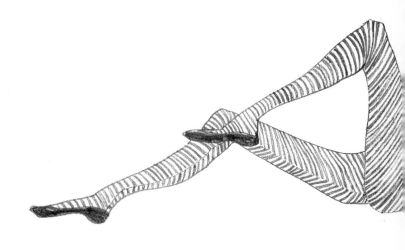

ZEBRA

Ze end.

First published in the UK in 2011 by
Apple Press
7 Greenland Street
London NW1 0ND
www.apple-press.com

ISBN 978 1 84543 400 7

First published in Australia by Penguin Group (Australia), 2010
250 Camberwell Road, Camberwell, Victoria 3124, Australia
(A division of Pearson Australia Group PTY Ltd)

Penguin Books Ltd, Registered Offices: 80 Strand, London WC2R 0RL, England

1 3 5 7 9 10 8 6 4 2

Cover and text design by Ortolan, ortolan.com.au
Illustrations by Kat Macleod

Colour reproduction by Splitting Image, Clayton, Victoria
Printed and bound in China by 1010 Printing International Limited